A Home for the New Nation

By Joyce A. Barnes
Illustrated by Marc Scott

CELEBRATION PRESS
Pearson Learning Group

Contents

Chapter 1

★ ★ ★ ★ ★ ★

Important Work to Do

Sarah Clark carefully crossed the bridge over Rock Creek. She didn't want to drop her basket of pecan pies. She was on her way to the Federal camp in George Town.

3

As Sarah entered the woods, she heard a tree trunk crack. A tall oak was falling to the ground, and someone yelled, "Progress!" When the tree hit, it shook the earth under her feet. Sarah knew why the trees had to come down.

It was a cool March afternoon in 1791. The United States was two years old and still had no capital city. So President George Washington had chosen land along the banks of the Potomac River, between the states of Virginia and Maryland, for the new Federal District.

Many people were working to help the president build a grand capital city. Some measured the land. Others cut down trees to make way for new buildings and streets.

Sarah's favorite worker was Benjamin Banneker, one of the surveyors. These men measured out each mile and placed a stone to mark it.

Mr. Benjamin was the smartest person Sarah knew. He could measure the land by looking at stars. She found him near his tent. "Hello, Mr. Benjamin!" she called.

"I saved you a slice of pecan pie," the young girl said.

Mr. Benjamin smiled. "Mmm! Your mother's pies are the best I have ever tasted."

Major Andrew Ellicott, the man in charge of the surveyors, rode up on his horse.

"Benjamin," the major said, "can we look over your latest numbers? Pierre L'Enfant has given the president a report about his plan for the city. I'll meet with President Washington tonight at Suter's Tavern."

Mr. Benjamin said, "Certainly, Major."

Sarah's face fell. She had been looking forward to a reading lesson with Mr. Benjamin. Still, she knew that her friend had important work to do.

She waited as the major got down from his horse and hurried into one of the tents. Then she said shyly, "I wish I could help you build the new city, Mr. Benjamin."

Benjamin Banneker chuckled. "Sarah, you keep selling those wonderful pies. Let us worry about building the capital city."

Sarah walked on with her basket of pies. As she sold the tasty slices, she thought about what the major had said. There was a meeting that night with the president. It would be at Suter's Tavern, where Sarah's mother worked.

"I'll find a way to go to that meeting!" she said to herself.

Chapter 2

A Plan for the Capital

Sarah ran to the tavern after she had sold all the pies. She found her mother cooking in the kitchen. "Mama," she cried, "the president is coming here *tonight*!"

Her mother smiled. "You want to see the president, do you? Well, I think I can arrange that, Sarah. Most likely we'll need some help if a big group is coming here."

That evening, Sarah served cider to the president himself!

"I have here a report from Pierre L'Enfant," said the president. "His ideas are very grand! He wants long, wide streets and fine views."

"That sounds *too* grand," said one man. "We must keep some land to sell!"

"The capital city must not be sliced into pieces of land to sell!" Major Ellicott said.

Sarah could see that the major was angry. She guessed that he liked Pierre L'Enfant's ideas for building the capital.

Another man spoke up. "L'Enfant's plans will put a street through my new house!"

Sarah's mother had told her which of the men was Thomas Jefferson, the secretary of state. With a laugh, Jefferson said, "L'Enfant has very firm ideas."

Finally, the president rose to speak.

"Gentlemen," he said, "I am glad to know your thoughts. We can talk more after L'Enfant starts to sketch his ideas." He bowed and walked away.

The other men finished their cider. Then, one by one, they left the room. Only Major Ellicott stayed.

"You can come out of your corner now, Sarah," Major Ellicott teased her.

"Oh, sir," said Sarah. "Are you angry?"

"Not with you, child," he replied. "I *am* concerned. Pierre L'Enfant's grand city deserves to be built the way he wants it."

Sarah and her mother walked home together. Her father was waiting for them.

He looked tired from his farm chores, but he was smiling. "Your friend came by," Papa told Sarah. "Said he had a gift for you!" Papa held out a sheet of paper.

Sarah took the paper and carried it over to the candlelight. "It is the letters of the alphabet!" she cried. "Mr. Benjamin wrote them out for me."

"What a kind man," Mama said. "I'll bake him a whole pie tomorrow."

Chapter 3

A Stargazing Lesson

Rain fell for days. Mr. Benjamin could not measure land, because he couldn't see the stars at night. Sarah still took pies to camp every day.

16

Now Mr. Benjamin had some time each day to teach Sarah how to read. She took her cousin John along.

"The skies have cleared," Mr. Benjamin said one day. "It is time you had a stargazing lesson."

That evening, Sarah, John, and their families made the long walk back to the camp. Mr. Benjamin asked the group to sit on blankets on the ground.

"Look overhead. Find the stars that form the big water dipper," he said.

Mr. Benjamin showed them that the dipper was part of a star pattern called the Great Bear. He taught them that the Sun was a star, circled by Earth and other planets. His words made Sarah's heart beat faster.

In late April, the borders of the Federal
District were finally all marked and cleared.
It was time for Mr. Benjamin to go home.

"I don't want you to leave," Sarah told
Mr. Benjamin. "Will you write to me? I can
read now."

He took Sarah's hand. "I must go home to my farm in Maryland, but I will write to you, Sarah."

Sarah smiled, but then her face fell. "Who will tell me of the plans for the capital city?"

Major Ellicott rode up. "Benjamin, I wish you a safe journey home. Please give my regards to your neighbors, my cousins. How can I thank you for your good work?" he asked warmly.

Mr. Benjamin smiled. "If you happen to see Sarah at the tavern, Major, would you be kind enough to tell her of the progress of the capital city?"

"I will do that," the major promised.

Sarah tried to hide her tears as Mr. Benjamin mounted his horse and rode away. She would miss her friend.

Chapter 4

★ ★ ★ ★ ★ ★

News

Major Ellicott kept his word. Whenever he saw Sarah helping her mother at the tavern, he told her how the plans for the city were coming along.

"I have something to show you, Sarah!"
he said one warm September evening. From
his pocket, the major pulled out a drawing.
"Pierre L'Enfant has given the president
his final plan for the new city," Major
Ellicott told her. He showed her a sketch.

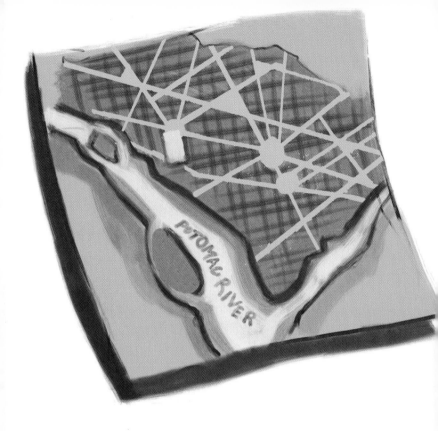

The major showed her where the president's house would be built and where Congress would meet. Wide avenues stretched out from the buildings.

I wish I could live in the new city, Sarah thought.

That night, Sarah told her parents what Major Ellicott had said about the new city.

"Perhaps the city would be a good place to open our bakery," Mrs. Clark said. "We've almost saved enough money. The clay jar is nearly full of coins."

"Mama!" Sarah cried. "How wonderful!"

"Mr. Suter will miss Mama at the tavern," her father said, "but we must think of our future. Maybe we *should* move to this new capital city."

Sarah's wish was going to come true!

Chapter 5

The Grand City

The Clark family worked as hard as they could in the months that followed. They saved every coin. In February, a letter came for Sarah from Mr. Benjamin.

> Bannaky Springs Farm, Maryland
> February 1792
>
> Dear Sarah,
>
> I send good wishes to you and your family. I am well. I am busy playing my violin and studying the stars. What is more, I have published an almanac. That is a book filled with useful facts.
>
> I plan to visit George Town soon. I wish to give a copy of my almanac to an old friend. I will look for you at Suter's Tavern.
>
> Your faithful friend,
> Benjamin Banneker

The next time Sarah helped her mother at the tavern, she saw Major Ellicott.

"Has work begun on the president's grand house?" she asked shyly.

The major shook his head. "Pierre L'Enfant has been very stubborn, Sarah. He even tore down a rich man's house because it was in his way! In fact, the president told him he couldn't work on the city plan any longer. What do you think Major Pierre Charles L'Enfant did *then*?"

"What?" Sarah asked.

"He refused to give his map to us," said Major Ellicott. "The president has asked me to create it all over again!"

"Oh, my!" Sarah said. "I will leave you to your important business, sir."

Sarah helped Mama with her cooking. It was a busy night at the tavern.

She thought about Major Ellicott's words. *What if the major cannot make an exact copy of the city plan?* she worried. *What will happen to the fine new capital city then? Oh, the city must be built the way Pierre L'Enfant planned it! It must!*

As Sarah left the tavern that night, she heard someone say, "Sarah!" It was Mr. Benjamin. Sarah hugged him.

"Have you heard what is happening with the plan for the city?" she asked. She told him all about the problem.

Mr. Benjamin frowned. "I must send word to the major that I can help. I know the exact measurements of the new city."

"He is inside the tavern!" Sarah cried.

"That is very good news. Thank you, Sarah!" said Mr. Benjamin.

Not long afterward, the Clarks moved to a place near the Potomac River in the new city. Their bakery was a great success. One day, Sarah heard a customer say, "Did you hear that Major Ellicott's plan for the city has gone to the engravers?"

"Yes, and they say his plan was very close to L'Enfant's own map," said his friend.

Sarah smiled. She pictured Mr. Benjamin helping the major to recall L'Enfant's ideas.

L'Enfant's plan became the model for the beautiful city of Washington, D.C. The wide avenues were just as the talented and stubborn L'Enfant had planned them.

As for Benjamin Banneker, he visited the Clarks' bakery whenever he came to Washington. Sarah always had a slice of pie ready for her friend.